Four Pals™ in Science Class

(An Adventure with Friends who are Different)

By Angel Tucker

and

Robert A. Rohm, Ph.D.

Illustrated by Steve Pileggi

Personality
INSIGHTS
PRESS

Four Pals™ in Science Class

By
Angel Tucker
and
Robert A. Rohm, Ph.D.

Illustrations by Steve Pileggi
Editors, Nancy Marbry and Shirley Voorhees
Graphic design by Pedro A. Gonzalez

Published by

Personality INSIGHTS PRESS

Printed in the United States of America

ISBN: 978-0-9841121-4-2

ACKNOWLEDGMENTS
for "Four Pals"™ Series 1

First, I'd like to thank God, who is the creator of ALL things – including our personalities! Psalms 139:14 says that we are all "fearfully and wonderfully made" and "marvelous are thy works!" I'm so thankful that He made us all different! Just think how crazy the world would be if we were all the same!

Next, I'd like to thank my husband, Dennis, for being so supportive of the development of these books and encouraging me when I thought they would never get finished! Also, to my four children, who have kept me from ever having a dull moment! I love and appreciate each of them!

I want to thank Madison for her input and excitement about the books from an 11 year olds' point of view. She is a blessing!

A huge thank you to Steve Pileggi, illustrator of this series, for his creativity and ability to make the stories come alive! Much was asked of him, in a very short period of time, and he came through with flying colors! He is truly amazing!

Last, but certainly not least, words cannot even begin to express my thanks to the Personality Insights Team for seeing my vision for these books and committing to countless hours of hard work and editing to make the "Four Pals" series a reality. Many children will benefit from their selfless efforts! A special thanks to Dr. Robert Rohm, Nancy Marbry, Shirley Voorhees, and Pedro Gonzalez. Their individual talents have been invaluable in this project! God Bless them!

Angel Tucker
C.H.B.C
National Christian Speaker
Author
Proverbs 3:5-6

When writing a children's book series such as this, you face several challenges: First, you want each book to be simple and easy to understand. Second, you do not want any child to feel labeled or "put down," rather you want them to feel encouraged and "lifted up." (The entire D-I-S-C Model of Human Behavior is not about what is wrong with you – it is a wellness model – it is about what is right with you!) Third, you want each child to gain understanding of how to grow to be a well-balanced person using the traits from all four personality styles. In a word, you hope the books are educational.

I believe, with the help and efforts of the dedicated team of people who put these books together (Angel Tucker, Nancy Marbry, Shirley Voorhees, Pedro Gonzalez, Steve Pileggi, and myself) that we have achieved all of the above goals. I hope you will agree!

Robert A. Rohm, Ph.D.
Personality Insights, Inc.
Atlanta, GA
www.personalityinsights.com
1-800-509-DISC (3472)

Welcome to the "Four Pals"™ Series!

These books were created for three reasons:

1. To show children that God is the creator of everything – even our personalities!
2. To teach children all about the different personality types!
3. To let children know that it's okay to feel unique and special as well as be different from their friends!

Here is a further description of each of the personality types. This should assist you in giving your children a better idea of how God made each of us different. The important fact to remember is that all children have a unique blend of ALL FOUR of these personality styles. No one will fit neatly into one style. All children will possess some of all of these traits and will exhibit each of the four different types of behavior at different times. Usually, however, one style will emerge as the most predominant trait and this will be the trait the child will demonstrate most often. It will also be the trait that he or she will be most comfortable using on a daily basis. We often say, "That is the way they are wired!"

David

DAVID is our wonderful "**D**" type personality! The letter "**D**" represents the word "**Dominant**." "**D**" type personalities love to be in charge and have things done their way. "**D**"s think fast and move fast! Their communication style is bottom line. Their attitude is lead, follow, or get out of my way! You never have to wonder what a "**D**" is thinking – they will just tell you! "**D**" children are usually the ones leading all the group activities and telling all the other kids what they will be doing. God bless the **Outgoing/Task-Oriented** "**D**" type personality!

For more great tips on understanding the D-I-S-C child, please get a copy of *A+ Ideas for Every Student's Success* at www.personalityinsights.com or www.personalityprofiles.org

Iris

IRIS is our wonderful "**I**" type personality! The letter "**I**" represents the word "**Inspiring**." "**I**" type personalities love to have fun! They are very optimistic and outgoing! They tend to be forgetful at times because they are usually in a hurry to do things! They also move fast! Their communication style is exciting and enthusiastic. They don't do well with lots of details and information and may have difficulty accomplishing tasks because they lose their focus. They love being around other people, thrive on attention and love to entertain others! God bless the **Outgoing/People-Oriented** "**I**" type personality!

Summer

SUMMER is our wonderful "**S**" type personality! The letter "**S**" represents the word "**Supportive**." "**S**" type personalities are very compliant and pleasant. They do not like conflict. They like peace and harmony. They sometimes have trouble making decisions because they tend to make up their minds slowly. Their communication style is "easy-going." In other words, they tend to adapt easily to whatever is going on around them in their environment. They love people and relationships! "**S**"s love being around other people and helping everyone they meet. They are sensitive and sometimes get their feelings hurt easily. They like to feel appreciated and secure. God bless the **Reserved/People-Oriented** "**S**" type personality!

Charlie

CHARLIE is our wonderful "**C**" type personality! The letter "**C**" represents the word "**Cautious**." "**C**" type personalities enjoy having a routine and schedule. They are usually very good students and like things that challenge their mind. Their communication style is A to Z, which means that, details and planning are very important to a "**C**." That is why they ask so many questions. The "**C**" type personality prefers to do things that have been planned out especially if it involves a large group of people. They are very comfortable being alone and working independently. They appreciate quality more than quantity. God bless the **Reserved/Task-Oriented** "**C**" type personality!

The "**Four Pals**" series is designed to have 1 book in each series that highlights each of the four different personality styles. There will be 4 more books released in the future.
www.personalityinsights.com/fourpals or www.personalityprofiles.org

Charlie was so excited! Today was Monday and his Science Teacher was going to make the announcement. Today Charlie would find out what each student would be making for his or her Science Project.

Charlie loved Science! It was his favorite subject in school, although he really liked Math and History, also. He was hoping that the project would require lots of thought and research. Charlie loved to learn and enjoyed doing projects that taught him different things.

Finally, it was time for Science class. "Okay class," his teacher Mrs. Dixon said, "Each of you are going to build a volcano. You have until next Monday to complete your project. Then the other teachers will decide which one is the best. The winner will receive a trophy."

Charlie couldn't believe it. A volcano? This was going to be great! He couldn't wait to get started!

His friends, who were in his class were also excited about the project, but for different reasons. They each had their own idea of how to make a great volcano! Each one of them was anxious to get started on the volcano project right away.

After school, David and Iris rushed to their homes to get busy. They both figured they could get their volcano done in only a few days. Each of them liked getting things done quickly, except that sometimes Iris would forget what she was supposed to be doing! After all, her favorite thing to do was to play with friends. She would have to make sure that she didn't forget to finish her project!

Summer checked to see if anyone needed help with their project before she went home to start on hers. Summer loved helping other people. She was very sweet.

Library

Charlie did not head home. He headed for the Library.

He wanted to make sure that everything about his volcano was correct, so he had plenty of learning to do before he started. He knew it would take him the entire week to get it just right.

David was the first to start on his project. He didn't think it was necessary to read any books on volcanoes. He knew what a volcano was supposed to look like, and that should be good enough. One thing was for sure. He wanted to build the BIGGEST volcano in the class!

Iris was the next to start on the project. She also thought it was a waste of time to read about volcanoes. She didn't really like reading anyway, unless it was books that were funny. She loved things that were funny! Iris knew right away what she wanted her volcano to look like. She wanted to make the most colorful one in the class!

Summer decided that she should probably do some research before she started her project. It took her a while to decide whether to go onto the Internet or to go to the Library and check out some books. Sometimes Summer had trouble making decisions.

After thinking for a long time, she decided to see what she could find on the Internet.

Meanwhile, Charlie was still doing research. Lots and lots of research. He didn't even start building his volcano for three days. He was going to make sure it was just right! He knew he could win that trophy.

Before they knew it, it was Monday and time to turn in their volcano projects. Every child came in with their volcano covered up. The teacher was going to let each of the students take a turn showing everyone their project.

First, it was David's turn. David proudly pulled the cover off his project and revealed a three foot volcano!

"Isn't it huge?" he said. "I bet it's the biggest one in the class!" "It is quite large," Mrs. Dixon agreed. David was very happy that he had indeed built the biggest volcano in the class.

Next, it was Iris' turn. She squealed with excitement as she threw the cover off of her project. All the other children, and Mrs. Dixon were very surprised by what they saw.

It was a volcano alright, but it was very different. Iris' volcano was pink, red, green, blue, and orange. It had purple lava painted at the top and it also had an umbrella! "Well, that is certainly colorful," said Mrs. Dixon. "I know, isn't it great?" exclaimed Iris in delight!

The teacher asked Summer to show everyone her volcano next. Summer politely said, "Yes ma'am." She then carefully took the cover off her project.

Summer had made a volcano that had trees and flowers around the bottom. She had also painted a stream going in front of the volcano.

"I wanted to make sure the animals had a place to live," she explained. "That is a very good idea," replied Mrs. Dixon. Then Mrs. Dixon gave Summer a big smile! This made Summer feel very special and she was so thankful that her teacher liked her project, too.

Finally, it was Charlie's turn. He took the cover off his project to reveal the most perfect volcano ever. It looked just like a picture! Charlie had researched exactly what materials were usually found on a volcano and he duplicated them the best he could. He also made his volcano ooze a red substance that looked just like real lava!

All the other kids in the class thought it was great, and Mrs. Dixon was very impressed!

"You did a fabulous job!" said Mrs. Dixon. "You must have spent a lot of time on your project," she added. "Yes," replied Charlie. "I spent 15 hours on research alone. I even wrote a book report to go along with the project," he replied. "I really loved learning so much about volcanoes!" he said.

It was then time for the teachers from all the other classes to judge the volcanoes. It was no surprise to anyone that Charlie won. All the friends agreed that his was definitely the best!

"You know, Charlie," said David, "this reminds me of a verse in the Bible that says, 'Every man will receive his reward according to his own labor.' Your reward was the trophy!"

"I guess you're right," replied Charlie. And all the friends agreed. They were happy that Charlie won and they each looked forward to their next adventure together.

Reader's Guide

This is Book 4 in this series. The focus in this book is on Charlie the **Cautious "C"** type personality! To get all four books in the "Four Pals" series go to the website: www.personalityinsightsights.com/fourpals or call 1-800-509-DISC (3472)

David

Was it apparent to you that David simply wanted to get the project done as quickly as possible? There is nothing wrong with David wanting to get his work completed quickly. However, sometimes the important thing is to get the work done correctly, not quickly. Some things take time and David is usually in a hurry in just about everything he does. David likes "big" and "fast" rather than "small" and "slow"! David is not afraid to be different and he is willing to take a risk. He is a self-starter who has the potential to achieve great things in life.

Iris

Have you noticed that Iris has a difficult time learning to focus? It is not because there is anything wrong with her. She has a good mind. She simply has a short attention span. On one hand she is popular, fun and lighthearted. On the other hand this may cause her to have difficulty studying and making good grades at school. Since school occupies so much of Iris' time it is very important for her to understand her own personality style. If she takes the time to listen and focus her energy in the right direction she will do better in school. The school environment can "make or break" Iris.

Charlie

Could you tell that Charlie was right at home when it came to issues relating to subjects such as math or science? This is because Charlie is a thinker! He loves to use his mind. Out of all the different personality styles, perhaps Charlie's style fits best in the school environment. No one enjoys learning new things or figuring things out more than Charlie. His inquisitive nature makes him a joy and delight to most of his teachers. Also, many of his teachers have a similar personality style. That is why they often connect in the classroom. Charlie is a very bright individual and has the potential to succeed in everything he does in life.

Summer

Summer loves to please her teacher and this time is no exception. She also likes to help her friends in school. Summer is usually a good student because she wants everything to remain peaceful and stable in her environment. She really dislikes conflict. It upsets her to the point that she may "shut-down". Did you notice in this story how Summer not only completed the task, but she thought about the well-being of the environment? She was also concerned about how the animals might be affected by a volcano. Summer is thoughtful about everything and gets along well with everyone.

About the Authors

Angel Tucker is a wife, mom and national speaker/trainer. As a Certified Human Behavior Consultant and owner of Personality Profiles, LLC, she has been speaking and training professionally across North America for the past 18 years. She began by teaching churches and youth groups. She instantly knew it was her desire to share this life changing information with as many people as possible. Angel and her husband Dennis, who is an officer in the United States Air Force, have four children – Danielle, Chase, Hannah and Elijah. When Dennis retires, they plan to travel the country together – teaching and training others about our wonderful God-given personalities!

If you are interested in having Angel speak at your next engagement, please contact her using the following information:

Website: www.personalityprofiles.org
Email: personalitypro@msn.com

Dr. Robert A. Rohm is a renowned National and International speaker. He has traveled all over the world including every continent (except Antarctica), teaching and training people in the D-I-S-C Model of Human Behavior. Most people consider Dr. Rohm to be one of the leading authorities in the world on understanding personality styles and relationship dynamics.

Dr. Rohm has been an educator for over 40 years. He has earned 5 college degrees and has written or co-authored over 20 books and over 350 published articles. He also has numerous audio and video training programs.

Dr. Rohm is a father and grandfather and believes that has been the true source for many of his insights and learning experiences. He has entertained and enlightened audiences for many years. His mixture of stories, illustrations, and humor make him a gifted speaker to audiences of all ages!

Dr. Rohm is also the co-founder of discoveryreport.com

To learn more about Dr. Robert Rohm or have him at your event, go to: www.robertrohm.com or www.personalityinsights.com or call Personality Insights, Inc. at (800) 509-DISC (3472)

The "Four Pals" series is designed to have 1 book in each series that highlights one of the personality styles.
There will be 4 more books released in the future.
To find out more go to:
www.personalityinsights.com/fourpals
or
www.personalityprofiles.org

Watch for our next "Four Pals" Series 2:

Four Pals at the Pool
Four Pals at the Circus
Four Pals in a Parade
Four Pals on a Field Trip

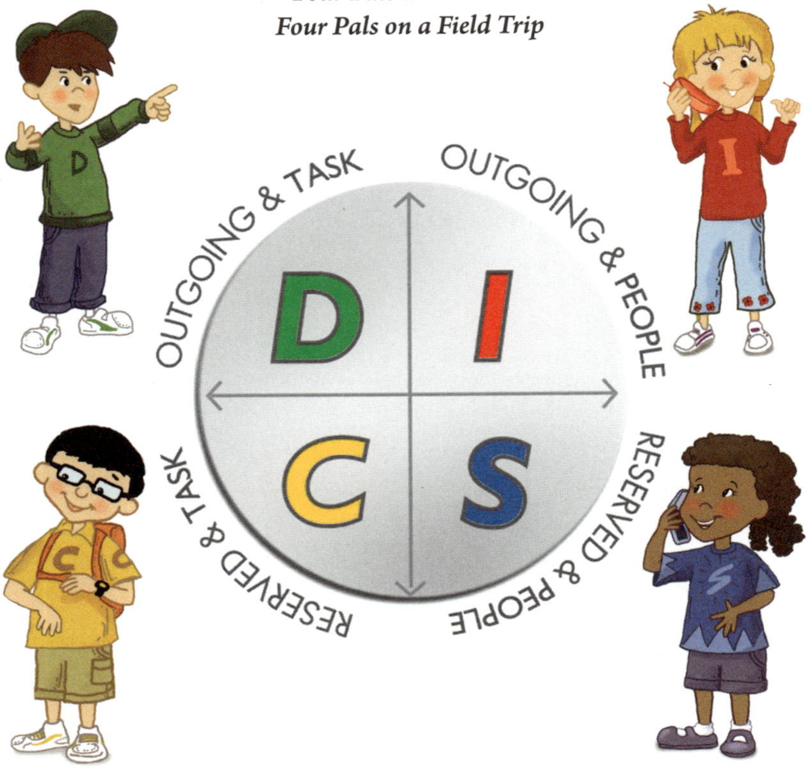

For more in-depth understanding of personality styles visit us:

For an autographed copy visit Angel Tucker at: www.personalityprofiles.org

www.personalityinsights.com
or contact us at:
Personality Insights inc.
P.O. BOX 28592 Atlanta, GA 30358-0592
800.509.DISC (3472)
info@personalityinsights.com

Personality
INSIGHTS
PRESS